"Shaken is an engaging, well-designed, extremely helpful and accessible resource that can help any young person take more control of their emotional lives, especially while in the midst of struggle, without adding shame or guilt to their circumstance. As we begin to emerge from the Covid19 cocoon, teenagers and young adults will be scrambling to try and figure out how to navigate life's re-entry. SHAKEN presents a powerful and timely tool fo

Chap Clark, PhD. *Author, Hurt 2: Inside the World of*

"Too often, resources for youth work are either creative, or they ha
rare in that the excellent content (specifically helping struggling tee
by the extremely creative approach. I'll look forward to using this with teens going through hard times."

Mark Oestreicher, *speaker and youth ministry trainer.*

"Shaken' is a really helpful resource for young people and youth groups as they think about how to handle the stresses of life in healthy ways. Packed with gospel wisdom and practical advice, it's creative, accessible and even fun. The workbook section is especially useful as young people seek to apply the truths they're learning to their own situations."

Emma Scrivener, *author, blogger and speaker.*

"The Big House are experts on walking with young people during difficulty, so who better to resource young people providing an innovative way of discovering how to cope when life shakes us. Shaken demonstrates how faith is relevant to us when we face difficulty. It allows us to have open conversations about living well when life shakes us and how we can discover who God is in those moments. This resource celebrates the uniqueness of each young person, providing an interactive workbook for young people who are looking to stand Unshaken".

Christina Baillie, *Diocesan Youth Officer in Connor Diocese.*

"SHAKEN will encourage a movement of young people to live with boldness, courage and faith. Acknowledging that we all have good and bad days, SHAKEN is designed to help young people to manage their more challenging emotions with practical and healthy coping mechanisms. This journal is hope-filled and hope-fuelled by the Gospel and has an incredible message to share: No matter what happens that tries to shake you, with God's help, you too, can be unshaken! Want to encourage a young person to live life to the full? Then make sure you get SHAKEN in their hands NOW."

Dr Claire Rush, *Vice-President of The Girls' Brigade International.*

SHAKEN

We, like dice, get shaken sometimes. Something tricky happens and **we don't know what to do, or how we feel.**

Thankfully, we have more control over how we land than dice do. The life we live and the choices we make can change whether we land and live well, or struggle after being shaken.

This resource is designed to **help you live well when life shakes you.**

THIS IS YOUR BOOK!

NAME:

GOOD
DAYS
& BAD
DAYS

All of us experience good days and bad days – **this is normal!** When things feel tricky or difficult, we do things to try and deal with how we are feeling. Sometimes we know we are doing this, sometimes we don't.

The things we do to try and deal with our feelings are called **coping mechanisms.** There are two types of coping mechanisms. Healthy ones, and unhealthy ones. The healthy ones help us to land well when we are shaken. The unhealthy ones don't. In fact, they can end up making you feel worse and making life more difficult.

So **choosing healthy ways of coping is really important** – they will help you live as well as you can no matter what shakes you in life.

THIS BOOK... Wants to help you find healthy coping mechanisms that work for you and which help you live well. You are uniquely made and loved by God, and there will be a way for you to uniquely cope with the difficult things in your days. **Help and hope is here for you!**

SHAKEN

LET'S GET STARTED

This is **your book!** You can write, doodle on it – it's yours.

You can read it **on your own – or with others.** It's up to you!

We think it works well when you do both. Some of you will find it hard to sit on your own and work out what helps you to deal with tough things. Others of you will find it hard to say what you think in a group. We think a little bit of each is really helpful as you discover healthy ways to cope.

IT'S A BOOK AND A GAME?

Yes! This is how it works.

We have given you a **20-sided die** (who knew they existed?!) Roll it and let it decide which healthy coping mechanism you are going to try out. The number it lands on is the coping mechanism you are going to try. You can do this on your own or with friends.

When you have **tried it,** have **a think or chat** about whether you liked it, what it felt like to do, and decide if it might help on a difficult day. We've included space for you to **write your thoughts** on each page, and you can give it a **score out of ten!**

We've got some **young people, like you, to try out lots of our coping mechanisms.** They've shared some of their reviews towards the end. It helps us know that we are all created differently and can use different healthy coping mechanisms in our lives.

We wonder **which will top your favourites list** at the end of the book!

Will you and your friends have the same or different healthy coping mechanism?

BEFORE YOU PLAY

We want to introduce you to three really important things that will help each one of us to cope and live well in our good and bad days.

Talking
Listening
Spotting.

These three things, added together with your unique ways of coping will help make you feel healthy and full of life. **No matter what you face in life!**

TALKING...

Is how we let other people know us and how we know other people.

It is part of God's design for us to live well!

For some people, it is hard to say the things they think or feel. For others, it is easier. But most people find it difficult to talk about things that make them feel sad or hurt. Some things will make it easier to talk. We will help you with that – because talking is a really important part of learning how to cope and live well in life.

GETTING READY TO TALK!

YOU are important to God. **YOU** are worth knowing. **YOU** have value. What **YOU** think and feel is really important. So pick who **YOU** share **YOUR** thoughts and feelings to carefully.

HERE ARE OUR TOP THREE TALKING TIPS TO HELP YOU GET STARTED.

 1. WHO WILL LISTEN?

Can you think of a friend, parent, grandparent, aunt, uncle, teacher, youth leader, school nurse, school counsellor or another adult you trust who might love to listen to how you are feeling?

If it is hard to think of this person, why don't you start with God? He is always listening and loves to listen to you. Tell Him how you are feeling. Ask Him to show you a good person to talk to.

You don't have to talk to God in a certain way, or a certain place. You can talk to him on your own in your room, out for a walk, as you write or draw your feelings down. God knows you, understands you and is ready to listen. He wants to hear about the little and big things in your life.

WHAT DO YOU WANT TO SAY?

You might have something in your life that seems really big to talk to an adult about, or something that feels smaller. Both are really worth talking about. Sometimes it helps to think about what you want to tell someone. You could write it down or draw what you want to say. Bring this with you if you are meeting up with someone to talk. Or have it beside you when you talk to them on the phone. It will help you say it out loud. And if it is too hard to say the words, you can just give the person what you have written and they will still hear you.

 ## YOU'VE SAID IT, WHAT NEXT?

When you speak to someone you trust, we hope that they listen well to you – you deserve to be heard! Sometimes people are great at listening and sometimes they aren't. If the first person you try doesn't listen well, don't give up. Try someone else.

And remember, sometimes when your friend or an adult has really listened to you they might need to include another trusted adult in to help. Hard as it might seem, trust that they are looking after you if they say they need to do this. They should always chat with you about this though, before they get more help. There are times it can really help to have more than one adult involved and helping.

"God's there, listening for all who pray,
for all who pray and mean it."

PSALM 145:18 (MSG)

LISTENING...

We've thought about talking being really important in learning to cope and live well. The next really important thing we want to tell you about is listening!

LISTENING IS AMAZING.

- We can be **encouraged** as we listen.
- We can **understand** others and ourselves more.
- We can **discover** new ways of thinking and being.
- We can **lose feelings** of aloneness and hopelessness.
- We can **build** relationship.
- We can make someone else feel **heard, important, valuable.**

HERE ARE OUR TOP THREE LISTENING TIPS!

 1.

LISTEN TO OTHERS WHO UNDERSTAND WHAT YOU ARE GOING THROUGH

As you talk to adults you trust, be ready to listen to their response to you. Listening to the life stories and experiences of other people can be such a gift!

But remember this! Only listen to **someone you trust and who is coping and living in healthy ways**. Finding these people can be hard. But start with the people you, or your trusted listener, already know and trust. That will help you build a safe network of people who can help you. But listening goes beyond those who have heard our stories too.

Often when something feels hard in life, we can feel alone or that no-one understands what we are going through. Hearing other people's life stories can help us to feel connected with others. While you and your life story is unique, others might have a similar story and similar feelings. Your trusted listener (or listeners) might know someone who has gone through a similar experience as you, and who has found healthy ways of coping with the experience.

You might also want to listen to trustworthy people with similar stories. Why not ask your trusted adult to help you find people who have shared their stories online? As you hear their stories, it can help us feel less alone or that someone else understands where we are coming from. As you hear of other people's experience you might also learn some new healthy ways of coping with your difficult situation.

This will help you make healthy choices in coping and to feel encouraged and supported by others.

 ## 2. LISTEN TO OTHERS WHO LOVE GOD

A guy called David wrote the book of Psalms in the Bible. He went from conquering a giant as a small boy, to becoming a great King of a mighty nation. Throughout David's life he had many highs and lows, celebrations and total muck ups. Maybe this combination of good and bad times is something you know too?

In the ups and the downs of his life, David wrote the book of Psalms. As we read the Psalms (or listen on an app!), we hear his thoughts and feelings. We hear how honest he was with God, how he told God everything. That included his sadness, loneliness, fear, despair, anger, doubt and inner darkness, and then his relief in finding God's care, his gladness and thankfulness to God. David had some really hard experiences. He also discovered how good, forgiving, and constantly loving God was to him. David discovered God was closely with him (Psalm 145 is just one example of this).

David is a great guy to listen to. We think he will help you learn more about talking to God about everything that is going on in your life. And we think it will encourage you to hear that someone else had feelings you might have

⁶ Your marvellous doings are headline news;
I could write a book full of the details of your greatness.

⁸ God is all mercy and grace—
not quick to anger, is rich in love.
⁹ God is good to one and all;
everything he does is suffused with grace.

¹³ Your kingdom is a kingdom eternal;
you never get voted out of office.
God always does what he says,
and is gracious in everything he does.
¹⁴ God gives a hand to those down on their luck,
gives a fresh start to those ready to quit.

¹⁹ He does what's best for those who fear him—
hears them call out, and saves them.
²⁰ God sticks by all who love him,
but it's all over for those who don't.

PSALM 145: 6, 8-9, 13-14, 19-20 (MSG)

(overwhelmed, hurt, sad, betrayed, abandoned, scared) and what they did with those feelings. If David could learn how to talk and listen to God in the hard and good days of his life, so can you! God hasn't changed. He will listen and help us today just as he listened and helped David!

As you listen to David's words, you might even find they are a great description of how you feel and what you want to say. If you find that, use them! Tell God you feel like David did and use his words to help you say it. Write them out. Paint them. Use them in whatever way feels helpful!

LISTEN TO JESUS

 Jesus is important because he was fully God and fully human. He shows us what God is like, what is important and helps us understand Him more. Jesus' friends on earth made sure that the things He said and did were told to many people and written down so as they would be remembered. We can learn what Jesus is like as we hear these stories. As we listen to how Jesus was with people, we will be encouraged.

- He **listened** to those who came to Him, young or old, no matter who they were

- He **stopped and listened**, even when he looked busy.

- He listened, **saw** and **understood** people's difficulties.

- He treated each person with **kindness** and helped them.

- He treated people with **respect** and **valued them.**

- He **forgave** and **healed** people.

- He **included** people who others had left out.

- He offered people **rest** and **no pressure.**

- He **changed situations** that looked impossible.

Not only did Jesus help other people in their tough days, Jesus had difficult situations of his own to cope with. This is what he did:

- **He asked** his friends to help him.

- **He talked** to God about his feelings, and the difficult situations.

- **He asked** God for help.

- **He listened** to the help God gave.

- **Jesus trusted God completely,** even when he felt alone. Even when it looked like God had abandoned him.

Jesus trusted God even in His darkest, hardest days. We listen to Jesus as we see God's power revealed by Jesus' miracles in the lives of so many, helping them to see hope for their lives.

When God brought Jesus back to life, it was to make sure that we can be close to God and have hope. Hope, no matter what we face in life. Certainty that at the right time God will bring an end to the pain, sadness, aloneness, hopelessness, and tears that can make so many people's days difficult.

As a way for you to explore listening to Jesus, why not look through Mark 1:29 - 2:17? This book was written by Mark, one of Jesus' friends. Spend some time reading through Jesus' teaching and pick out two things which are relevant to your life. That's one example of how to listen to Jesus!

Some days you feel great. Other days you don't 100% but aren't sure why. It might be like butterflies in your tummy or a fuzzy head. On these days (unless you've eaten a butterfly or bumped your head), it is a good idea to try and spot your feelings.

There is something going on in you that needs understood and listened to. **We want to spot our feelings to understand** and stop our butterfly tummies or fuzzy heads from staying around.

INVESTIGATE:

- When did you start to feel like this?
- What had just happened?
- Can you think of a word that describes your feeling?

Asking these three questions and giving yourself time to think about the answer can help you understand a bit more about yourself and what you are feeling. There are no right or wrong answers. It is ok to feel what you feel.

If you can start to understand when, or why you started to feel the way you do it will help you understand what you are feeling. It also works that if you can describe what you are feeling, then you can work out what happened to make you feel like that!

Spotting and understanding our feelings is really important. What we do with our feelings will change us and our lives. Everybody has to learn how to understand and spot their feelings if they want to cope in healthy ways and live their life fully.

We have included a chart on the next page which might help you spot and describe your feelings.

Over the next week, try and take the time to spot your thoughts and feelings. You might want to do this once a day or at regular times throughout the day. Try and find a word to summarise your feelings, or draw what you are feeling in this chart (we've given you some ideas to get started but you will have even more!).

This activity isn't about getting the 'right' feeling– it is about spotting what feelings you are having.

Suggested words:

safe / secure / valued / included / excited / cheery / happy / loved

tired / hopeful / worried / nervous / withdrawn / pressured / lonely

stressed / angry / ignored / low / empty / hurt / scared / hopeless

anxious / relaxed / left out / supported

If you spot difficult feelings in **more than two of your days,** it would be a good idea to try some healthy coping mechanisms to help...and top of our list in this is to tell someone how you are feeling !

You could even show them this chart to help you explain what you have been feeling.

SPOT IT CHART!

	WHEN I WOKE UP	DURING THE DAY	AT BEDTIME	EXTRA THOUGHTS?
SUNDAY				
MONDAY				
TUESDAY				
WEDNESDAY				
THURSDAY				
FRIDAY				
SATURDAY				

COPING...

We've got that talking, listening and spotting are all important. Now it is time to think about your unique and healthy coping mechanisms!

We want to find healthy coping choices that we can use as soon as our feelings are beginning to overwhelm us. These are in the moment choices. They will help you to deal with your feelings positively, and begin to relieve them. You might find different choices helpful in different situations, and with different feelings.

We also want to find healthy coping choices that we can use over a longer time. These are planned choices. Planned choices help you to cope and live well through difficult situations, and feelings, that last longer. They also help you to prevent as many moments where you are overwhelmed by painful feelings.

As you grow in your understanding of your feelings, and which choices to make in coping with them, you will enjoy the life God has given you more and feel more fully yourself.

In the next part of this book, we have ideas for you to try in the moment and some planned choices. Give them a try regardless of how you are feeling and see what helps you! Remember, different choices can work in different situations for different people – the important thing is to learn what works well for you!

IN THE MOMENT...

Something has happened and suddenly you feel overwhelmed, or upset. Or maybe you feel angry, scared or very sad. Here are some ideas of what you can do in these moments.

Each of these ideas uses a part of you – your voice, your hands, your body, your mind. God has made you wonderfully, and He has given you the beginnings of how to cope really well in tricky moments.

1. SAY NO

If someone is asking you to do something you do not want to do, or is telling you that you have to do it – say **NO.**

If someone is hurting you or making you feel uncomfortable by what they are saying or doing – say **STOP.**

If you ever have to do this, please tell an adult (or adults) you trust that you've had to say no or stop. As soon as you can.

By telling an adult (or adults) you trust, it gives them the opportunity to support you and encourage you for being brave. You are very precious and no one should ever hurt you or force you to do something you feel scared or hurt by.

YOUR REVIEW:

SHAKEN IN THE MOMENT

YOUR RATING:

21

2. TALK

Could you phone a friend or trusted adult?

It can be really helpful to speak with someone who cares about you, right in that overwhelming, difficult moment. It helps you to remember that you are not alone. And it gives you a chance to express your feelings safely and before they grow bigger.

If you can't talk to a friend or trusted adult, would it help to phone **Childline**? You can phone Childline on 0800 1111 and chat about anything that is worrying you. Lots of young people phone Childline everyday to chat. You can also chat online with Childline. Go to **childline.org.uk/get-support** and click on 1-2-1 chat.

It is always better to talk about your worries than to keep them in, so get chatting!

- David spoke to Jonathan (1 Samuel 18:1)
- Jesus spoke to his disciples (Mark 14:34)
- Samuel spoke to Eli (1 Samuel 3:18)
- Mary spoke to Elizabeth (Luke 1:44)

Talk

YOUR RATING:

3. PRAY

God is always with you, and always ready to listen. He has seen all that has happened, and understands. In any moment you can talk honestly with Him – tell Him how you are feeling, ask Him to help you in that moment. **Here are some examples of what you might like to say, but you can pray in any way you want to:**

- Jesus, you are called Prince of Peace, would you give me your peace now as I am feeling anxious. **(Isaiah 9:6)**

- Jesus, you are called Wonderful Counsellor, would you come and be my comfort and counsellor now please. **(Isaiah 9:6)**

- Jesus, you calmed storms, please calm this storm in my heart and mind. **(Matthew 8:23-27)**

- Jesus you helped anyone who asked you to in the Bible, so please do the same for me and help me now.

Pray

YOUR
RATING:

25

4. MOVE

Moving can help break an intense or difficult moment. God made us with awesome bodies.

If you feel stressed or panicky, can you go for a walk? Or run? Could you take someone with you? Could you go and play football? Trampoline? Dance? Teach yourself to cartwheel?

In tricky moments, moving can help stop overwhelming feelings from growing.

Move

YOUR
RATING:

5. FRESH AIR

Getting outside and fresh air can help break a stressed moment. It can help you calm down and gather your thoughts to work out what you are going to do next.

If you are in school or youth group you will need to ask before you go outside. But if you tell the adult in charge why you want to get fresh air, they will be able to help.

When you get outside **notice what is around you** – the trees, the clouds, the rain, the sun. God created this world for us to enjoy **(Genesis 1:1)**. God is bigger than all these, and able to help you in this moment **(Isaiah 45:5-6)**. This moment will pass, and you will be able to get help. The difficult feelings can be reduced, they can be helped, and they also, can pass.

Fresh Air

SHAKEN IN THE MOMENT

YOUR RATING:

6. BREATHE

It is not as silly as it sounds!

Sometimes we need to pause what we are doing, and let our whole body breathe properly! It can help to calm your body and settle stressed or racing thoughts.

The Bible even talks about how it is helpful for us to take these moments to stop and be still, remembering who God is and that He is with us **(Psalm 46:10).** When we stop, and practise breathing slowly it can help us manage our stressful or panicky thoughts and feel more in control. There are lots of different breathing exercises you can try; **here is an example:**

> Begin by slowly inhaling and then slowly breathing out. Counting as you breathe: Breathe in through your nose for 4, hold for 6, breathe out through your mouth for 8. This technique allows more oxygen to fill your lungs, which can have a relaxing effect. As you breathe, you can also pray, "Jesus be my helper"

"Step out of the traffic! Take a long, loving look at me, your High God, above politics, above everything. Jacob-wrestling God fights for us, GOD-of-Angel-Armies protects us." **PSALM 46:10-11 (MSG)**

YOUR REVIEW:

Breathe

SHAKEN IN THE MOMENT

YOUR RATING

7. MAKE SOME NOISE

Some people find it helpful to make some noise, or listen to music when they are feeling upset. It is another way of expressing yourself and getting your feelings out!

You might want to put on your favourite upbeat song that makes you smile to dance around your room. Why not sing as loud as you can? Or stomp your feet? Maybe play an instrument you love? Or shout loudly where you won't disturb others? It is better to express your feelings than keep them in!

YOUR REVIEW:

**SHAKEN
IN THE
MOMENT**

YOUR
RATING:

8. STRESS BALL

Some people find it helpful to have busy hands when they feel stressed or anxious. You could try and make yourself a stress ball and see if busy hands help relax your mind!

How to make a stress ball: you can use a balloon, stretch it out, fill it up with flour using a funnel. You could cut the top off a bottle to use as a funnel too. Then remove as much air as possible, tying the balloon tightly at the top. Now you've got your own stress ball!

Stress Ball

SHAKEN
IN THE
MOMENT

YOUR
RATING:

9. CREATE

Painting, building lego, colouring, crafting, moulding clay, model building, writing...all of these (and there are more!) are examples of being creative. And each of these is a way in which we can break the intensity of tricky moments and help bring us calmly through them.

Which do you like doing? Or which could you try? Could you create something which reminds you that God loves you? Or shows you that God is in control?

YOUR REVIEW:

SHAKEN
IN THE MOMENT

YOUR RATING:

10. BLESS

Sometimes the most surprising, but helpful thing we can do when we feel overwhelmed by our difficult situation is to go and do something kind for someone else.

Maybe it is just helping someone with chores, or making something for someone. Writing a thank you note, or praying for someone. As we look to love and help others, it can help us remember that there is more to us, and our lives than our difficult moments.

As we consider how we can bless someone in our lives we follow the commands of Jesus when he says:

> "Let me give you a new command: Love one another. In the same way I loved you, you love one another. This is how everyone will recognize that you are my disciples—when they see the love you have for each other."
> **JOHN 13:34-35**

YOUR REVIEW:

Bless

SHAKEN
IN THE
MOMENT

YOUR RATING:

11. CRY

Most of us don't like crying and are embarrassed to. But sometimes the healthiest thing we can do when we are feeling hurt or overwhelmed is to cry and let those feelings out.

God made our tears so as we could cry when we needed to.

When Jesus' friend Lazarus died, Jesus saw Lazarus' sisters Mary and Martha and was overwhelmed with sadness. He cried with them (John 11:33-36).

It is ok to cry, it can be good to cry.

God sees every tear that you cry, and He understands how you feel.

> You've kept track of my every toss and turn through the sleepless nights,
> Each tear entered in your ledger each ache written in your book.
> **PSALM 56:8 (MSG)**

If you find that you are crying everyday, or can't stop crying please tell an adult you trust. Maybe you could tell someone in your family? Your teacher? Counsellor? Youth leader? Childline? GP? It is important to get help if this is how you are feeling.

Cry

YOUR RATING:

12. ENJOY

You may not feel like having fun, but actually taking a little time to do something you enjoy can help settle your worried mind, or upset heart when you have talked to God or someone else about your feelings.

You will have your own ideas, but here are two of ours!

BLOWING BUBBLES: Get a packet of bubbles or make some of your own using washing up liquid and water. Spend some time blowing bubbles. You could try and see how big a bubble you can blow. You might want to see how many bubbles you could get in one go.

LAUGHING: Take a moment to do something which will make you laugh, it might just be a little chuckle or a proper belly laugh! You could find the best joke you can and tell a few people. You could find a YouTube video which makes you laugh every time. Why not gather a few friends and tell funny stories together?

Laughing can be good for your body physically, decreasing stress hormones or releasing endorphins the body's feel good chemicals. It is ok for us to laugh, even when things are really tough.

Enjoy

SHAKEN
IN THE
MOMENT

YOUR
RATING:

PLANNED CHOICES...

So you've spotted that your feelings are uncomfortable, difficult – you might be sad, scared, angry, anxious, lonely, overwhelmed, or something else. But you do not feel happy.

We hope that you have managed to cope in a healthy way with your feelings in the moment they felt worst. Well done for trying to do this.

Now you are ready to make some more healthy choices to help these feelings improve, or become easier to cope with. We are going to suggest eight healthy choices that can add to our resources to give us all the best chance of coping well when life shakes us.

All of these choices are positive actions we can do. You can try them yourself or with others. Whatever works best for you!

13. TALK REGULARLY TO FRIENDS AND TRUSTED ADULTS

We thought about how to begin talking in our earlier section. Now we want to think about how to keep talking!

Talking regularly to friends and a trusted adult (or adults) is a really healthy habit to have. If you are in the habit of sharing your thoughts and feelings regularly it will be much easier to spot crisis feelings before they hit fully, and you will know that you are understood and not on your own in whatever is happening. Having at least one relationship like this is very healthy for everyone.

If you can think of a friend or trusted adult who you have this type of relationship with, then make it a habit to see and talk regularly. Don't be shy to ask to have time with them! If you can't think of a friend or trusted adult who you could regularly see and talk to, then ask God to give you this. And keep asking Him until he brings someone along!

God has made us to be known and understood in relationship, when we ask for His help in finding safe and healthy relationships, He will help us!

Talk Regularly

SHAKEN
PLANNED
CHOICES...

YOUR RATING:

14. EXPLORE COUNSELLING

Part of talking regularly to someone about your feelings and thoughts might include having a counsellor.

Counsellors are really good at understanding and helping people have healthy minds and hearts. They can help us understand our thoughts and feelings when they seem muddled and they can teach us new ways of looking after our minds and hearts. Because counsellors realise how helpful counselling can be in looking after your mind and heart, they all have their own counsellors too!

Your school might have its own counsellor. You can ask a teacher about this and how to get an appointment.

If you would like a counsellor who is Christian and you can talk to about God as well as your difficult situations, contact The Listening Space. It is our counselling service and an important part of The Big House.

You can visit **thebighouse.org.uk/listening** to find out more, and **@bighouseonline** to make an enquiry. You can also phone **028 9066 4300.**

YOUR RATING:

15. HAVE REGULAR TIME WITH GOD

"Don't fret or worry. Instead of worrying, pray. Let petitions and praises shape your worries into prayers, letting God know your concerns. Before you know it, a sense of God's wholeness, everything coming together for good, will come and settle you down. It's wonderful what happens when Christ displaces worry at the centre of your life." - **PHILIPPIANS 4:6-7 (MSG)**

We've encouraged you to talk to God in the moments where you feel overwhelmed or stressed and need help. It is also a really good idea to plan regular times of getting to know God, and talking to Him.

Some people take **time every day to read from the Bible** to learn more about what God is like. Doing this helps you to know what God thinks of you, and what is important to Him. It also shows you God's plan for how we can live really well and be full of life. As we grow in our knowledge of these things, we will find it easier to cope with difficult things when they happen and we will be quicker to remember that God is there ready to help us.

Some people also **take time to talk to God every day**, telling Him about their day, what they are feeling and asking for help. Maybe this is something you could try too?

Check out: some devotional apps for your devices. You could try Word For You Today or She Reads Truth/He Reads Truth. If you wanted an app to help with your prayer life, why not try 24/7 Prayer's Inner Room app.

You might even have **a friend who you could read the Bible and pray with.** You could arrange to meet every week to do this and you could both help each other to live as well and fully as possible!

YOUR REVIEW:

Time with God

SHAKEN
PLANNED CHOICES...

YOUR RATING:

50

16. EXPLORE WHAT JESUS SAYS ABOUT YOUR SITUATION

One of the best ways of knowing the God who made us and knows everything about us is to discover more about Jesus and what Jesus says.

Jesus shows us exactly what God is like.

We can find out more about Jesus by:

1. READING PARTS OF THE BIBLE

The Bible has lots of mini books in it – the mini books of Matthew, Mark, Luke and John show us what Jesus is like, what He does and what matters to Him.

If you feel lonely, you could explore these mini-books and find times that Jesus met someone who was left out by others. Find out what Jesus said and did for them. Jesus is the same today and will care for you in the same way. You might want to see how Jesus treated the unwell man in John 5:1-9, or how he acted towards Zaccheus in Luke 19:1-10.

Or if you are worried about someone in your family and really want God to help – find out what Jesus did when Jarius was worried about his daughter (Luke 8:40-56), or when Martha and Mary were upset about their brother (John 11:32-36).

These mini-books will also help us hear what Jesus says about us, our life situations and our choices.

They help us hear what Jesus says about us, love, worry, clothes, money, friendships, lying, cheating, judging, forgiving, living fully, healing and lots more!

2. SPEND TIME WITH, AND LISTEN TO SOMEONE WHO REALLY LOVES JESUS AND DOES WHAT JESUS SAYS.

You may need to search this person out, or maybe it is someone in your family. When someone really loves Jesus and does what He says, you will spot something special in this person – in some ways they will be like Jesus.

When we hear what Jesus thinks about us and our life situations, we have heard what God thinks of us and our life situations.

Knowing what Jesus thinks of us and our life will help us live well and to cope well when life shakes us.

> Jesus says: "Come to me. Get away with me and you'll recover your life. I'll show you how to take a real rest. Walk with me and work with me - watch how I do it. Learn the unforced rhythms of grace. I won't lay anything heavy or ill-fitting on you. Keep company with me and you'll learn to live freely and lightly."
> **MATTHEW 11:28-30 (MSG)**

YOUR REVIEW:

What Jesus Says

SHAKEN
PLANNED CHOICES...

YOUR RATING:

53

17. EAT, RELAX & SLEEP WELL

Our bodies, minds and hearts need given the right things to be healthy and time off that restores our energy and life. We also need to spot the things that stop us relaxing and remove them!

EAT: Let's start with what you can give your body – healthy food and drinks, and the opportunity to relax and sleep well. You can ask your trusted adult more about healthy food and drink choices.

RELAX: We all relax in different ways. It is good to learn how to relax and work out what helps you relax. Is it music? Relaxation techniques? Arts and crafts? Chatting to friends? What could you try as a new way of relaxing?

SLEEP: All of us need different amounts of sleep. Our minds and hearts need us to be asleep to help understand and cope with what has happened in our days. Our bodies need sleep to grow and be re-energized. So getting enough sleep is really important!

It can be hard to sleep if you feel worried or anxious. It can help to ask God to look after your worries for you and to help you sleep. It can also help to do something relaxing before you try to sleep.

Psalm 121 tells us that our 'Guardian God won't fall asleep. Not on your life!' Our Guardian God 'will never doze or sleep.' As we trust that God is looking after us - being our guardian, we can begin to relax to sleep. He will watch and look after us as we sleep.

A CHALLENGE!

Phones, TV, computers, in fact any screen alters our mind and makes it more difficult to relax and sleep. So it is really important to turn these off an hour before you are going to sleep. It is ok, and in fact healthy, to disconnect at times!

Do you think you could do this for a week? If you feel worried or anxious at the thought of this, spot the feeling and talk to your trusted adult (or adults) about it!

If you can spot an app that makes you feel stressed, why don't you delete it? Don't let your phone be in charge of how you feel!

Eat, Sleep & Relax

YOUR
RATING:

18. EXERCISE

It is healthy to have 60 minutes of physical activity every day. Physical activity helps us to feel better about ourselves, improves mood, sleep and grows energy. You can decide if you do this on your own or with friends or a trusted adult. Sometimes you will find it easier to chat to people as you do something active.

What do you like doing? Football? Netball? Trampoline? Walking? Roller blading? Running? Swimming?

You might also be able to explore this together with your friends – why not consider joining a local sports team or forming your own tournament? It might be an ultimate frisbee league or creating your own adaptation of a game?

YOUR RATING:

19. ENJOY

Plan something fun!

Having fun with someone you enjoy being with can be really helpful during busy, anxious or stressful times. So who do you like being with? What do you like doing together? Playing games? Sport? Getting ice-cream? Going to youth club?

Or maybe you would enjoy some time on your own? Reading a book? Learning a new skill? Making music? Making cookies?

Make a plan to do this soon - and to keep doing it regularly!

YOUR REVIEW:

Enjoy

YOUR RATING:

20. DREAM OF WHAT IS TO COME

> "God can do anything, you know—far more than you could ever imagine or guess or request in your wildest dreams! He does it not by pushing us around but by working within us, his Spirit deeply and gently within us."
> **EPHESIANS 3:20 (MSG)**

Moments pass. So can painful feelings, and difficult periods of time. Sometimes the difficult situation changes so that it is less difficult. Other times the difficult situation remains, but we change in it, or the help we have in it changes and how we feel in it then improves. There is hope in knowing this.

As we let hope enter in, we can begin to dream a little. Dream of what God might do in your life in the days and weeks and years that lie ahead. Ask God to give you His dream for your life. His vision of what your overwhelming moments, or difficult period of time can become.

Perhaps you could write your prayer down, or write your dream of what life could be down. Keep it and see what God has done after 6 months or even a year. You will be amazed at what can happen when we let God work His dream for our lives into reality.

Enjoy

SHAKEN
PLANNED
CHOICES...

YOUR
RATING:

These EIGHT PLANNED CHOICES are all things that will help you to live full lives, **no matter who you are, or what your days are like.**

If life has already shaken you with difficulty, these things can help you **feel steady** in whatever is going on.

If life hasn't shaken you yet, these things **will help you cope well and be unshaken** when difficult things do happen.

SHAKEN

FINAL THOUGHTS

SO WHAT DID YOU THINK?

Now you have played the game and tried some new ways of coping in tricky moments, what could work for you?

I LIKED THESE WAYS OF COPING IN THE MOMENT...

1

2

3

BECAUSE...

ASK YOURSELF:
- Which would work best most days or regularly?
- Which would work best in really difficult times?
- What works best over time?
- What works best in the moment?

I LIKED THE IDEA OF THESE PLANNED CHOICES TO HELP LIVE WELL...

1

2

3

BECAUSE...

REVIEWS FROM YOUNG PEOPLE LIKE YOU

STUART: I gave **PRAYER 9/10** as a coping mechanism because the ultimate comfort is knowing there is a God who loves you and who you can thank for everything. I feel more comfortable doing this alone so in that case it'd be 10/10 all the time. Also, I gave **EXPLORING WHAT JESUS SAYS ABOUT YOUR SITUATION 7/10** because although thoroughly comforting, I understand that for some people this can be seen as daunting and intimidating. This is not true. I encourage everyone to give this method a go.

ELLIE: My favourite was **TALKING TO A FRIEND** and I give it **10/10.** I think talking to someone always helps, it lets you vent and gets everything out but also lets you know you are not alone. Your friends can cheer you up or even just be a shoulder to cry on or cry with.

MYLES: I gave **PRAYER 6/10** as it is easy and convenient as you can do it anytime and anywhere. I also liked **ENJOY** as a planned choice and gave it **7/10.** It is fun to do things with people close to you and this could be good for people. I also liked **LAUGHING** in the unplanned choices as laughter is the best medicine!

FAITH: CONSIDERING WHAT JESUS SAYS about your situation, I gave it **5/10.** I think this one is quite hard to carry out as there is so many verses to choose from and hard to find one that helps your situation. I really enjoyed BREATHE and gave it **8/10** - this is very beneficial as it can put you in a calm mood and release the tension or pressure you have been carrying on your shoulders. I also really liked writing to myself through DREAM OF WHAT IS TO COME and gave it **9/10.** I think this is good because it helps you to realise what you want for yourself in the future whether its 5 months or 5 years. It can help you see what really matters and what you need to do to get to where you desire to be in the future.

EVIE: TALKING TO A FRIEND, I gave it **9/10,** as it really helps just off loading even if its' not about the subject. It just makes you feel better and it feels like a weight has been lifted off my shoulders.

MOLLY: I gave LISTENING TO OTHERS WHO LOVE GOD **8/10.** It allows you to see all the blessings that the Lord is giving you even in hard times. It reminds us that God is always there for us. Also ENJOY as a planned choice is good as it takes your mind off things and gives you something to look forward to, I gave it **9/10.** Blowing bubbles was also a good, fun, preoccupying activity.

LUCAS: We tried BLESS and I gave it **8/10.** For someone who is maybe having a rough time, putting the focus on someone else is always positive. As well as the general satisfaction of doing something for someone else, a random act of kindness makes you feel better about yourself and that's crucial!

Shaken?

Difficult things do, and will happen.
Difficult things may shake us,
but we don't need to stay shaken.

Because

God, who made us,
knows us, and loves us,
God who has seen all that
has happened
God who has seen what has
shaken us, is unshaken.

He is steady.
He is strong.
He is good.
He is kind.
He is able to help.
He wants to help.

And He will.
We just need to ask Him.

With God's help, you too
can be **UNSHAKEN.**
No matter what happens
that tries to shake you, you too,
can be **UNSHAKEN!**

"SHAKEN is a great resource from The Big House to support and navigate young people through difficult times - I have always believed that building resilience in young people is essential and will strengthen them on their own journey of faith as they grow with God. For youth workers, SHAKEN is a great resource to use to engage in meaningful conversations with young people, encourage them in their faith and challenge them too, all the while looking to the Bible and the example that Jesus set us."

Simon Henry, *Church of Ireland National Youth Officer*

"I love this hugely practical and creative resource to help young people stand firm when life shakes them. Use it on your own, find a friend to do it with or encourage your youth leader to use it with your youth group! It is aimed at helping you discover your identity in God and has healthy tools for you to try out as you endeavour to discover life in all its fullness through Jesus."

Gillian Gilmore, *General Secretary IMYC*

"What a timely and topically relevant resource for young people that is ideal for individuals or groups! With a variety of fun, practical, tried & tested ideas that aim to shape our faith, feed our emotions & strengthen us mentally, this workbook hopes to make; the difficult, simple; bad days, good; the shaken, unshaken!'

Phil Howe, *Training and Resources Manager, Scripture Union Northern Ireland.*

"A clear little gem of a booklet which offers help, information, but more importantly hope for young people navigating these strange times we live in."

Rachael Newham, *Author and Founder of Think Twice*

"Big House is one of those rare places that connects both practice and deep theological reflection. This ministry is a blessing to the church, the world and the young people it serves. I'm excited to continue to follow this ministry as it unfolds. It can teach us all a lot."

Dr Andrew Root, *Professor of Youth and Family Ministry at Luther Seminary, Minnesota.*